Who Was
J. R. R. Tolkien?

Who Was
J. R. R. Tolkien?

By Pam Pollack and Meg Belviso

Illustrated by Jonathan Moore

Grosset & Dunlap
An Imprint of Penguin Random House

To Pete Savage—we met in the wars—PP

To the ladies of Frodo's Kitchen—
because we love him, whether or no—MB

GROSSET & DUNLAP
Penguin Young Readers Group
An Imprint of Penguin Random House LLC

Text copyright © 2015 by Pam Pollack and Meg Belviso. Illustrations copyright © 2015 by Penguin Random House LLC. All rights reserved. Published by Grosset & Dunlap, an imprint of Penguin Random House LLC, 345 Hudson Street, New York, New York 10014. GROSSET & DUNLAP is a trademark of Penguin Random House LLC. Printed in the USA.

Library of Congress Cataloging-in-Publication Data is available.

ISBN 978-0-448-48302-3   10 9 8 7 6 5 4 3 2 1

Contents

Who Was
J. R. R. Tolkien?

Deep inside a
lonely mountain,
a dragon sleeps on
a mound of gold.
Suddenly, he wakes.
Someone has come to
steal his treasure! Only a great
warrior would do something
so brave and foolish. Who
dares to challenge him?

The burglar is brave,
but he isn't a warrior.
He is small and quiet,
and he has furry feet.
He is a hobbit.

Hobbits were born on a summer day around 1930 in Oxford, England.

Through the open window of his study in his house on Northmoor Road, Professor John Ronald Reuel Tolkien could smell the flowers outside as he sat at his desk grading papers. He was a professor of Anglo-Saxon at the famous Oxford University. He was an expert in ancient languages once spoken throughout Europe.

He did not earn much money, and Ronald, as he was called, had four children to support. So even though it was summer, he was grading School Certificate exam papers. These were the tests that all British students took when they were sixteen. Ronald earned extra money during his vacations by grading them. Ronald had already read dozens of student essays. But he still had more to read. He didn't have time to daydream.

Ronald's daydreams were rich and exciting. He loved to write stories about heroes in magical lands. They reminded him of the ancient myths that he loved as a child. When Ronald wrote, he didn't feel like he was making up stories. He felt as if he were rediscovering things that had once truly existed.

He turned a page in the essay booklet he was reading and found it empty. The student had left it blank. Without thinking, Ronald let his own pen scribble on the paper. He wrote: "In a hole in the ground there lived a hobbit."

In a hole in the ground there lived a hobbit.

Ronald didn't know what a hobbit was. He didn't know why it lived in a hole. But he was going to find out.

Chapter 1
Out of Africa

On January 3, 1892, John Ronald Reuel Tolkien
was born. Although his parents were English,
he was born in South Africa. Ronald's father,

Arthur, had come to South Africa to work at a bank. Ronald's little brother, Hilary, was born two years after him.

Life in South Africa was sometimes surprising. One day a neighbor's pet monkeys climbed into the nursery and stole some of Ronald's clothes. One afternoon young Ronald met a tarantula in the garden. Any day could offer an adventure.

In April 1895, Ronald's mother, Mabel, took
the boys on a long trip to her hometown of
Birmingham, England, to stay with her sister Jane.

Arthur had to stay behind in South Africa to work. He hoped to join them, but in November 1895, Arthur got sick with rheumatic fever. He couldn't make the trip.

By February, Arthur was still not well. Mabel and the boys planned to return to South Africa to be with him. On February 14, Ronald's nanny helped him write a letter to his father. Ronald thought that Arthur might no longer recognize him, he'd grown so much. But before Ronald had a chance to mail his letter, the family got a telegram. Arthur had died and was already buried. Ronald would never see him or South Africa again.

The family moved to the town of Sarehole, outside Birmingham. Ronald came to love the countryside there, especially the trees. For him, they were living beings, like very old people who had seen much in their lives.

Mabel taught the boys at home. She read
them lots of stories. Ronald liked the stories
about dragons best. He even wrote one of his
own when he was seven. Ronald thought that

stories of magic and knights and dragons were better than stories about people in his own time. They were more heroic and exciting. Mabel knew Latin, the ancient language once spoken in Rome. She taught it to Ronald. He was fascinated by the sounds that made up the strange words. They made him think differently about his own language. Where did words come from? Why did English sound different from other languages? When Ronald listened to stories or wrote his own, he thought about the words he was hearing as much as he thought about what was happening in the story.

In the spring of 1900, Mabel shocked her father by announcing she and the boys were becoming Catholics. Mabel's father was furious. Like many English people at that time, he didn't like Catholics. But Mabel stood firm. From now on, she and the boys were Catholic.

Ronald was now old enough to attend King

Edward's School, where his father had gone. The school was in Birmingham, so he had to take the train each day. On his way, he saw railroad cars with strange words on them, such as *Nantyglo* and *Senghenydd*. Ronald thought these words were even stranger than Latin. The words were

Welsh—a language spoken by the Celts, who lived in Great Britain long before. People in Wales still spoke Welsh, as well as English. The Welsh words on the boxcars reminded him of fairy tales and make-believe places.

The family moved to be closer to Ronald's school in Birmingham. They also found a new church, the Birmingham Oratory. One of the priests, Father Francis Xavier Morgan, became a good friend to the family. The boys needed a good friend. Mabel had developed diabetes and was very sick. On November 14, 1904, Mabel died.

Ronald was only twelve years old. And now both his mother and his father were gone.

Chapter 2
Love and Language

In her will, Mabel named Father Francis the guardian of ten-year-old Hilary and twelve-year-old Ronald. The boys went to live with their aunt Beatrice. Beatrice didn't mind that the boys were Catholic. Unfortunately, she didn't care much about the boys, either. Ronald was heartbroken to find she'd burned letters his mother had written without asking him.

At school Ronald became friends with Christopher Wiseman.

Ronald and Christopher were the two top students and shared a love of Latin and Greek. A teacher introduced Ronald to Anglo-Saxon, or Old English. That language became the English we speak today. Soon Ronald was reading one of the earliest recorded poems in Old English, *Beowulf.*

Ronald didn't just speak old languages; he studied the very structure of languages. During a school vacation, he experimented with creating a new language called "Nevbosh." Nevbosh was based on English combined with the Latin and French that Ronald was learning in school.

In early 1908, Father Francis moved both Tolkien boys into a boardinghouse. Ronald was sixteen at the time. One of the other boarders was a pretty nineteen-year-old orphan girl named Edith Bratt. Edith and Ronald often talked late into the night while leaning their heads out their windows. By the following year, the two had fallen in love.

BEOWULF
(DATED BETWEEN THE EIGHTH AND ELEVENTH CENTURIES)

BEOWULF IS THE OLDEST SURVIVING EPIC—OR HEROIC—POEM WRITTEN IN ENGLISH. THE FULL POEM IS 3,182 LINES LONG! IT TELLS THE STORY OF THE HERO BEOWULF. HE HELPS THE KING OF THE DANES DEFEAT FIRST THE MONSTER GRENDEL, THEN GRENDEL'S MOTHER. BEOWULF RETURNS HOME TO BECOME THE KING OF THE GEATS IN GEATLAND, SWEDEN, WHERE HE LATER DEFEATS A DRAGON.

IN 1936, J. R. R. TOLKIEN GAVE AN IMPORTANT TALK ON *BEOWULF*. HE FELT THAT CRITICS SHOULD PAY MORE ATTENTION TO THE POWER OF THE POETRY AND THE MAGICAL ELEMENTS THAN THE HISTORY BEHIND THE STORY. HE HAD SPENT MANY YEARS TRANSLATING THE POEM INTO ENGLISH. IN 2014 HIS VERSION WAS FINALLY PUBLISHED—AND IT BECAME A BEST SELLER!

Father Francis was worried about Ronald having a girlfriend, especially one who was nineteen! He moved the boys to a new boardinghouse. Ronald was upset. He kept thinking about Edith instead of studying for his scholarship exam. He was hoping to go to Oxford University that year, but Ronald failed the exam.

Father Francis wanted to make sure that Ronald went to a university. So Ronald was forbidden to even write to Edith until he was twenty-one. That was three years away. Ronald was heartbroken, but he didn't want to disobey Father Francis. Then one day he spotted Edith "sloshing along in a mac [raincoat] and tweed hat" down the street. Ronald couldn't resist stopping to talk to her.

They were caught! Soon Edith moved away to live with friends in another town. Ronald wasn't even allowed to say good-bye.

Without Edith, Ronald began to spend more time with his friends at school. He, Christopher Wiseman, Robert Quilter Gilson, and Geoffrey Bache Smith formed a group. It was called the T.C.B.S., or "Tea Club Barrovian Society." The boys met to drink tea and talk about poetry and language.

King Edward's held student debates in Latin.
In a debate, students choose different sides of a
problem, and each person argues against another
person. It teaches them how to think logically about
things. In one debate, the students presented their
arguments as if they were men living in ancient
Roman times. Ronald surprised everyone when,

pretending to be a visitor from Greece, he spoke
in Greek instead! Then he came in character as a
Goth—a member of an ancient barbarian tribe—
and spoke in Gothic! Gothic was a language
barely recorded, but Ronald had managed to learn
enough to impress everyone at the debate.

Ronald took the test at Oxford again, and this time he won a scholarship. Oxford is a world-famous university made up of many different colleges. Ronald would be going to Exeter College.

EXETER COLLEGE, OXFORD

Before he left for school, Ronald and Hilary went on a hiking trip in the mountains of Switzerland.

Ronald later talked about buying a postcard there. It showed an old man with a long white beard, a wide-brimmed hat, and a cloak. He was talking to a fawn. Ronald wasn't sure why he liked the postcard so much, but he always kept it.

Chapter 3
Oxford

At Exeter College, Ronald took classes on philology, the study of language and words. Most students at the university were from wealthy upper-class families. Everyone had a "scout" (a servant who waited on them). Ronald was not used to this kind of life! He was an orphan who had lived in a boardinghouse.

Ronald was still working hard to create his own language. As he worked on it, he wondered who might speak his made-up language. Latin had been spoken by the ancient Romans, who wore togas and rode chariots. Old English had been spoken by Anglo-Saxons, who drank mead made of fermented honey and fought with swords. Who would have spoken Ronald's language? Ronald imagined that his language was spoken by fairy folk in an imaginary world.

Ronald's T.C.B.S. friends went to Oxford or to England's other famous university, Cambridge. Most of the students at both these schools were men.

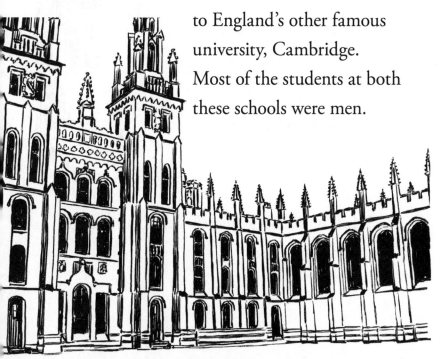

Ronald never had any contact with female students at Oxford. In January 1913, Ronald turned twenty-one. At the stroke of midnight he sat up in bed, grabbed a piece of paper, and started a letter. "Dear Edith," he wrote. "How long will it be before we can be joined together before God and the world?"

Edith wrote back that she was planning to marry someone else!

Edith explained that she didn't believe Ronald could still be interested in her after all this time. But Ronald had dreamed of Edith for too long to let her go that easily. He boarded a train and rushed to see her. Edith met him on the train platform. By the end of the day, she had agreed to marry Ronald.

There was one problem—Edith wasn't Catholic. Because of his loyalty to his mother and to Father Francis, Ronald wanted her to convert. So Edith became Catholic.

During the summer of 1914, Ronald traveled to Cornwall, in the southwest of England.

Cornwall's eerie, misty landscape made him think of the fairy folk he'd imagined speaking his language. At the end of his vacation, he went to see his aunt Jane. With visions of Cornwall still filling his head, he wrote a poem called "The Voyage of Earendel the Evening Star."

Ronald didn't realize it, but he had just taken his first steps in creating an entirely made-up world. Ronald would go on to write more stories about the imaginary place where Earendel lived, as if it were a real world with its own real history.

On August 4, 1914, Great Britain declared war on Germany. Most of Europe had been drawn into the conflict. The students of Oxford rushed to join the fight. Ronald's brother, Hilary, became a bugler, blowing his horn to call soldiers to their duty. Ronald trained for the army with the Officers' Training Corps at Oxford.

During Christmas 1914, the T.C.B.S. all got
together. They talked about how they longed to
make something lasting in the world, something
people would remember. Ronald was inspired to
write more about his fantasy world. But the next
time he would see any of his friends, it would be
on a battlefield.

WORLD WAR I

KNOWN AS THE GREAT WAR BY THE PEOPLE WHO LIVED THROUGH IT, WORLD WAR I STARTED ON JULY 28, 1914. WHEN THE ARCHDUKE OF AUSTRIA, FRANZ FERDINAND, WAS ASSASSINATED IN JUNE 1914, IT SET OFF A CHAIN REACTION. COUNTRIES WERE PULLED INTO THE WAR BY THEIR ALLIANCES WITH ONE ANOTHER. THEY FORMED TWO SIDES: THE ALLIES (WHICH INCLUDED GREAT BRITAIN, FRANCE, RUSSIA, AND LATER THE UNITED STATES) AND THE CENTRAL POWERS (INCLUDING GERMANY AND AUSTRIA-HUNGARY). ON NOVEMBER 11, 1918, GERMANY AGREED TO END THE WAR IN VICTORY FOR THE ALLIES. NEARLY NINE MILLION PEOPLE WERE KILLED DURING WORLD WAR I.

ARCHDUKE
FRANZ FERDINAND

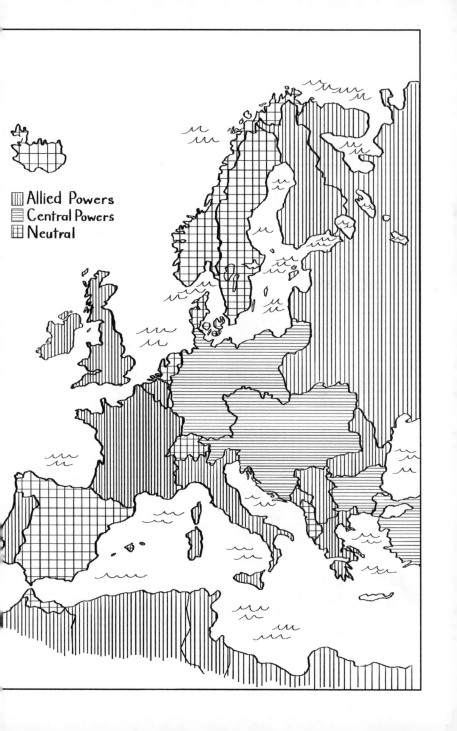

Allied Powers
Central Powers
Neutral

Chapter 4
In the Trenches

Ronald completed his studies at Oxford in June 1915. He graduated with the highest honors.

He entered the army as a second lieutenant. His specialty was signaling. That meant he would be near the front lines of the battle, passing signals to the other soldiers. He did this with lamps, flags, and portable telephones.

It was a dangerous job. Ronald had to go through a lot of training before he would be sent to war.

While Ronald was training at an army camp in Bedford, Edith was living in Warwick. Ronald bought a motorbike so he could visit her whenever he had time off. Ronald was still writing poetry. And he was even lucky enough to have one of his poems, "Goblin's Feet," published.

On March 22, 1916, Ronald and Edith got
married. Ronald waited until almost the last minute
to tell Father Francis the news. He thought the
priest would still be against the marriage. Instead,
Father Francis wished them the best. Ronald and
Edith had a short honeymoon in Somerset, in the
southwest of England. When they returned, Edith

moved to a village that was close to Ronald's army base. But almost immediately, on June 4, 1916, Ronald got orders that he was being sent to war.

On June 6, 1916, Ronald arrived in Calais, France. Three weeks later he joined the Battle of the Somme.

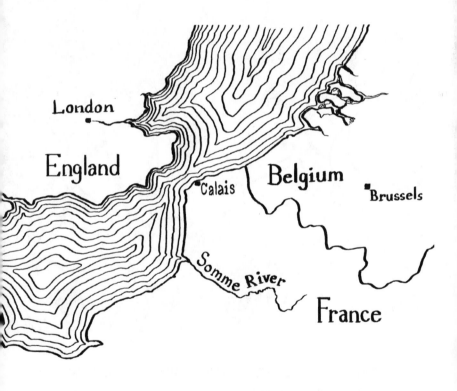

THE BATTLE OF THE SOMME

THE BATTLE OF THE SOMME WAS FOUGHT IN
FRANCE BETWEEN JULY 1 AND NOVEMBER 13, 1916.
IT TOOK ITS NAME FROM THE SOMME RIVER, WHICH
RAN THROUGH THE BATTLEFIELD. IT WAS ONE OF

THE BIGGEST, LONGEST, AND BLOODIEST BATTLES OF
WORLD WAR I, LASTING FOR OVER FOUR MONTHS.
OVER A MILLION MEN WERE WOUNDED OR KILLED
THERE.

Ronald's battalion was settled in a French village, where they waited for their turn to join the battle. On July 1, Ronald's friends Rob Gilson and Geoffrey Smith were part of the attack. On July 14, Ronald himself joined the fight.

World War I was fought with *trench warfare*. That meant both sides dug deep trenches that

stretched for miles. The ground in between the two sets of trenches was called *no-man's-land*. It didn't belong to either side. The men fought from inside the trenches, popping up to shoot over the top at the soldiers on the other side. A man who poked his head over the top was in danger of being shot. The trenches were surrounded by barbed wire.

Ronald and his company made the long march
at night through miles of mazelike trenches to
the front line. He found trenches filled with mud
that covered all the signaling machines. He could
only send signals with lamps or flags, because
the Germans had tapped the telephone lines and
could hear what the British were saying to each
other.

Worst of all, both the trenches and no-man's-land were full of the bodies of dead soldiers. Even the trees, which Ronald had always thought of as old friends, were black and dead.

Ronald spent three days with little sleep at his post in the trench. Many of the men in his company were killed trying to attack the German side. Finally, Ronald's company was sent back to the village for a rest. When Ronald stumbled into a hut to sleep, he found a letter from Geoffrey.

It was sad news. Rob Gilson had been killed.
Ronald wrote back to him, "I honestly feel that
the T.C.B.S. has ended."

Ronald's life settled into a routine: trenches,
attacks, and rest. He got used to the constant
explosions of shells and
to the sight of men
dying all around
him. He got used
to having lice—
tiny itchy bugs that
filled his uniform—
and to the rats
that infested the
trenches.

On August 19, Ronald met Geoffrey again.
They had dinner together before Ronald returned
to the trenches. So far he was not hurt, but he
knew he could be killed at any minute. In
October, Ronald came down with trench fever.

It was an illness carried by the lice that were everywhere in the trenches. On November 8, he was sent back to England, where he was reunited with Edith. They spent Christmas together in 1916.

During the holiday, Ronald got a letter from Christopher Wiseman. He told Ronald that their friend Geoffrey had been killed by an exploding shell.

Ronald reread a letter that Geoffrey had written him right before he died. In it he said, "May God bless you, my dear John Ronald, and may you say the things I have tried to say long after I am not there to say them, if such be my lot."

Chapter 5
The Storyteller

Ronald was never well enough to return to the front lines of the war. He felt strongly that he had a duty to keep his promise to his friends who had not survived. He wanted to create something lasting. He started writing stories about his fantasy world. His first story was called "The Fall of Gondolin." It was about a city where magical elves lived, and its destruction at the hands of the evil Morgoth and his armies. Ronald's elves were not cute little men. They were tall, beautiful, and wise. "The Fall of Gondolin" was full of romance, betrayal, and clashing armies—just like *Beowulf*, the epic poem that he loved so much.

Ronald and Edith returned to Oxford, where he had found a job working on the *Oxford English Dictionary*. It was the perfect job for Ronald, who had always loved words so much. Ronald also worked as a tutor, helping many of the new women students who were now going to Oxford.

On November 16, 1917, he and Edith had a son, John. The family took long walks together in the woods. On one walk, Edith started dancing under the trees. It inspired Ronald to write a story about a man, Beren, who falls in love with an elven princess named Lúthien. Since Lúthien was an elf, she would live forever—she was immortal.

OXFORD ENGLISH DICTIONARY

IN 1857, A GROUP OF FRIENDS WHO LOVED WORDS BEGAN A PROJECT TOGETHER. THEY DIDN'T LIKE ANY OF THE DICTIONARIES AVAILABLE AT THAT TIME. THEY DECIDED TO CREATE ONE OF THEIR OWN. THIS DICTIONARY WOULD RESEARCH EVERY WORD SO THAT PEOPLE WOULD KNOW WHEN IT FIRST APPEARED AND WHERE IT CAME FROM. FOR INSTANCE, IF YOU LOOKED UP THE WORD *DRAGON* IN THE *OXFORD ENGLISH DICTIONARY*, IT WOULDN'T JUST TELL YOU THAT A DRAGON WAS A MYTHICAL MONSTER. IT WOULD TELL YOU THE WORD *DRAGON* DATES BACK TO THE MIDDLE AGES AND CAME FROM THE GREEK WORD *DRAKON*, WHICH MEANS SERPENT.

THE FIRST FULL DICTIONARY WAS PUBLISHED IN 1928. THE SECOND EDITION WAS PUBLISHED IN 1989. IT WAS 21,728 PAGES LONG!

Beren was mortal. He was a simple human who would die one day. It was called "Tale of Tinúviel."

In the summer of 1920, Ronald was offered a teaching position at Leeds University in England. That October, the Tolkiens' second son, Michael, was born.

Edith liked life at Leeds. She made friends with the wives of the other professors. Ronald and another teacher, E. V. Gordon, translated the ancient poem *Sir Gawain and the Green Knight* together.

Ronald and Gordon started a club at Leeds. Its members were professors and students who loved to read Old Icelandic sagas—stories from northern Europe in the eleventh to thirteenth centuries. They called themselves the Viking Club.

SIR GAWAIN AND THE GREEN KNIGHT

THIS POEM WAS WRITTEN IN MIDDLE ENGLISH, A TYPE OF ENGLISH THAT PEOPLE SPOKE SOMETIME BETWEEN THE 1100S AND THE 1400S. IT IS A STORY OF LOYALTY, HONOR, AND ADVENTURE.

SIR GAWAIN WAS ONE OF THE KNIGHTS OF KING ARTHUR'S ROUND TABLE. IN THE POEM, HE IS CHALLENGED BY A GIANT GREEN KNIGHT DRESSED IN GREEN, RIDING A GREEN HORSE. SIR GAWAIN CHOPS OFF THE KNIGHT'S HEAD, AND THE GREEN KNIGHT PICKS IT UP AND RIDES AWAY WITH IT. NOW GAWAIN MUST MEET THE KNIGHT A YEAR LATER AND HAVE HIS OWN HEAD CHOPPED OFF. BUT GAWAIN IS NOT GOING TO GO DOWN WITHOUT A FIGHT.

They made up songs in Anglo-Saxon. Ronald became one of the most popular professors at Leeds.

In 1924, Ronald and Edith had another son, Christopher, who was named after Christopher Wiseman. The next year, Ronald got word that a teaching position had opened up at his old university, Oxford. It was a professorship in Anglo-Saxon. Ronald was thrilled to get the job.

During his last summer at Leeds, Ronald took his family to the seaside on the northern coast of England. One day Michael lost a toy dog.

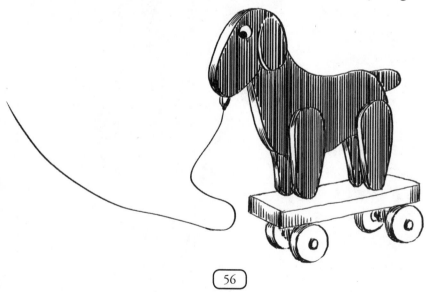

To make him feel better, Ronald wrote him a story about a toy dog named Rover. The little story grew and grew to include a wizard, a dragon, a sand-sorcerer, and a trip to the moon. He gave the story the heroic name of *Roverandom*.

Chapter 6
The Inklings

In early 1926, Ronald was working at his new post as a professor at Oxford. There, Ronald met another young professor. His name was Clive Staples (C. S.) Lewis, but everyone called him Jack.

C. S. LEWIS (1898–1963)

C. S. "JACK" LEWIS WAS BORN IN IRELAND. LIKE J. R. R. TOLKIEN'S MOTHER, JACK'S MOTHER DIED WHEN HE WAS JUST A BOY. AND LIKE TOLKIEN, HE FOUGHT IN WORLD WAR I, WHERE HE WAS WOUNDED IN 1918. HE WAS A TEACHER AT OXFORD AND ALSO A WRITER. TOLKIEN'S CHRISTIAN FAITH WAS A HUGE INFLUENCE ON LEWIS. THIS CAN BE SEEN IN THE CHRONICLES OF NARNIA SERIES. PUBLISHED BETWEEN 1950 AND 1956, THEY ARE LEWIS'S MOST POPULAR BOOKS, HAVING SOLD MILLIONS OF COPIES WORLDWIDE.

C. S. LEWIS

Jack loved ancient myths as much as Ronald did. Growing up, he and his brother, Warnie, who also lived in Oxford, had created their own imaginary world. Jack wanted to hear more about Ronald's imaginary world. What did he call it? Ronald named his world Middle-earth.

Edith was not as happy at Oxford as Ronald. She spent her time at home with her three sons and a daughter, Priscilla, born in 1929. Edith didn't get along with the wives of the Oxford professors. She felt like they were all more educated than she was. It made her sad when Ronald spent his spare time with friends, rather than his family.

Ronald and Jack had started meeting with some other friends twice a week. They called themselves the Inklings. When they got together, they shared the stories and poems they were writing.

Around 1930, Ronald started writing a new story. It was set in Middle-earth. But instead of being a story about romantic elven warriors and princesses, it was about a hobbit. He was named

Bilbo Baggins. Like all hobbits, he was small and never traveled far from home. He lived in a hobbit-hole under a hill called Bag End—named after the farm where Ronald's aunt Jane now lived. One day Bilbo was visited by a wizard named Gandalf. Gandalf had a long white beard, a tall, pointed hat, and a long cloak, just like the man on the postcard Ronald had found in Switzerland.

Ronald's children loved hearing about Bilbo's adventures. So did some of his Oxford students. So did the Inklings, especially Jack.

Ronald and Jack had a lot in common. But there was one thing about Jack that Ronald couldn't understand. He wasn't a Christian. He believed in God, but not the stories of the Bible. Ronald couldn't understand how his friend could doubt anything in the Bible. One night after a meeting, Ronald and Jack took a walk with another Inkling, Hugo Dyson.

Ronald and Hugo told Jack that to them the story of Christianity was just as amazing as the Icelandic sagas they loved. But it was a true story. For the first time, Jack understood what Christianity meant to Ronald. Soon after their talk, he converted to the Church of England.

By 1932, Ronald had almost finished *The Hobbit*. For years it sat in a drawer. What Ronald didn't know was that a former student of his, who now worked for a book publisher, was talking about *The Hobbit*. Her name was Elaine Griffiths. Years earlier she had read her professor's unfinished story. She couldn't forget it. Elaine decided to show *The Hobbit* to her bosses at the publishing house. She had no idea that she was opening the door to a whole new world.

Chapter 7
The Hobbit

Stanley Unwin was one of the heads of the publishing house George Allen & Unwin. He gave *The Hobbit* to his ten-year-old son, Rayner.

Rayner earned one shilling (about ten cents) for writing a book report on it. According to him, the story would appeal to all children between the ages of five and nine. His father trusted Rayner and decided to publish the book.

The Hobbit was published in September 1937. Jack wrote a glowing review of it for the *Times*. The book sold out quickly. In the United States, Houghton Mifflin made plans to publish it. Allen & Unwin wanted a sequel—

a story about what happened next. Ronald had written many stories about Middle-earth. But when he showed the publishers a collection called *The Silmarillion*, they turned it down. Those stories were too grown-up.

Ronald tried to write about a new hobbit, Bingo Bolger-Baggins. But the more he wrote, the less the story sounded like *The Hobbit*. It was too scary and too adult. Even the Inklings agreed.

At this time, most people thought stories about magic and imaginary places were only for children. Ronald didn't agree. In 1939, he wrote a lecture, "Fairy Stories," about the importance of fairy tales for everyone. Ronald decided to write his new story for adults. The main character became Bilbo's young cousin, Frodo Baggins.

The story was sometimes scary and included imagery that seemed to recall the trenches of World War I.

BRITAIN, FRANCE DECLARE WAR

That same year, the world once again went to war. Ronald's children were now almost grown up. John was studying to be a priest. Michael had joined the army. Christopher was at Oxford, where Jack Lewis taught. Priscilla was still in school.

Ronald was assigned to be an air-raid warden. When he was on duty, he spent the night patrolling the streets. He was making sure that

everyone had their lights off. Keeping towns dark
meant that enemy planes would not find them.

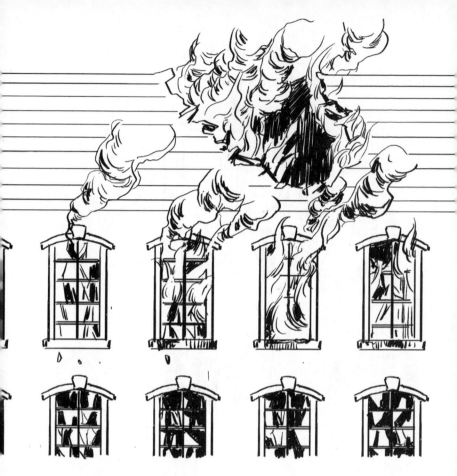

Although no bombs were dropped in Oxford,
the city of London was attacked often. On
one night in 1942, a bomb started a fire in the
warehouse where Ronald's publisher held all the
copies of *The Hobbit*. The books were destroyed,

and it remained out of print until after the war.
The publisher had no new books to sell.

But by then, *The Hobbit* had already sold so
many copies that soon Ronald no longer had to
grade papers in the summer to earn extra money.

In 1943, Christopher joined the Royal Air Force and went to train in South Africa. Ronald was still working on his sequel to *The Hobbit*. He sent his son new chapters as he wrote them. Of all Ronald's children, Christopher was the one who best understood the made-up world his father had created.

When the war ended in 1945, Michael got married and had a son, also named Michael. Christopher returned to college and became a member of the Inklings. By now, Jack Lewis had become a famous writer. His many books included a trilogy set in outer space. He was also becoming well-known for lecturing about Christianity and speaking on the radio.

In 1949, four years after the end of World War II, Ronald finished his second book. He called it *The Lord of the Rings*. It had taken him twelve years to write. The question was: Would anyone read it?

Chapter 8
The Lord of the Rings

Rayner Unwin, the boy who had earned a shilling reading *The Hobbit*, was now a student at Oxford. Ronald gave him a copy of his new book to read. Rayner found it "weird" but "brilliant and gripping." He thought his father should publish it.

Ronald wanted to publish *The Lord of the Rings* along with other stories of Middle-earth. But that didn't happen. Years went by. Finally Ronald agreed to let Allen & Unwin publish just *The Lord of the Rings*.

The story was so long, they decided to split it into three books. The books were called *The Fellowship of the Ring*, *The Two Towers*, and *The Return of the King*. The three books together were known as *The Lord of the Rings*.

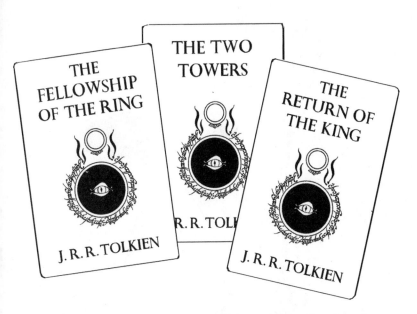

Right away, Ronald could see that the books weren't going to look like he had imagined. He wanted the inscription on the magic ring printed in red ink, but it was too expensive. Ronald argued with printers who tried to change the spellings of his words: It was *dwarvish*, not *dwarfish*, and *elven*, not *elfin*! Ronald insisted on including detailed maps of his world in the books. Christopher Tolkien, who was now married and also an amateur mapmaker, drew the maps for his father.

The first book, *The Fellowship of the Ring*, was published in England in July 1954. By then Jack Lewis had taken a job teaching at Cambridge. But he wrote a great review of the book in *Time & Tide* magazine. *The Fellowship of the Ring* was published in October in the United States. In November, the second book, *The Two Towers*, was published in England, and in the United States shortly after.

Some reviewers thought that it was silly to write a book for adults with elves and dwarves and magic. But the books sold well. The publisher printed 3,500 copies, and they quickly sold out. Sales in the United States were just as strong. *The Two Towers* ended with the heroes in a dangerous situation. People couldn't wait for the third and final volume.

But the last book wasn't finished yet. Ronald hoped to include a lot of background information about Middle-earth. It would take time to gather it together. Ronald was now receiving fan mail for his work, and he often answered letters instead of working. For readers dying to know what happened next, the wait was terrible!

It wasn't until October 20, 1955, that the final volume of *The Lord of the Rings* was published. It was called *The Return of the King*. As fans were rushing to read it, Ronald was giving a lecture on ancient languages. He had no idea how much the books were about to change his life. The quiet professor was about to become a worldwide star.

THE LORD OF THE RINGS

IN *THE HOBBIT*, BILBO BAGGINS FINDS A MAGIC RING. HE PASSES IT DOWN TO HIS COUSIN, A HOBBIT NAMED FRODO, WHO IS UNAWARE OF THE RING'S POWER. *THE LORD OF THE RINGS* TELLS THE STORY OF THE TRUE POWER OF THE ONE RING AND THE QUEST TO DESTROY IT.

THE WIZARD GANDALF VISITS FRODO AND EXPLAINS THAT THE CREATOR OF THIS RING, THE EVIL SAURON, WILL STOP AT NOTHING TO RECLAIM IT. SAURON WANTS TO USE THE RING'S EVIL POWER TO GAIN CONTROL OVER ALL THE PEOPLES OF MIDDLE-EARTH.

WITH THE HELP OF "THE FELLOWSHIP"—TWO OTHER HOBBITS, TWO MEN, A DWARF, AN ELF, AND GANDALF—FRODO AND HIS FRIEND SAM GAMGEE SET OUT TO RETURN THE RING TO WHERE IT WAS CREATED: A VOLCANO IN THE LAND OF MORDOR. IT IS ONLY INSIDE THE VOLCANO THAT THE RING CAN BE DESTROYED. WHILE FRODO AND SAM JOURNEY TO MORDOR, THE REST OF THE FELLOWSHIP BATTLE SAURON'S ARMIES.

THE LORD OF THE RINGS IS A STORY ABOUT FRIENDSHIP AND BRAVERY. TOLKIEN'S CHARACTERS SHARE HIS LOVE OF NATURE. THE HEROES HAVE A VERY POWERFUL WEAPON—THE MAGIC RING. BUT THEY ARE NOT INTERESTED IN ITS POWER. THEY ONLY WANT TO DESTROY THE RING, SO THAT IT CANNOT BE USED BY ANYONE FOR EVIL PURPOSES, AND TO RETURN TO THE SHIRE—THEIR HOMELAND IN THE COUNTRYSIDE.

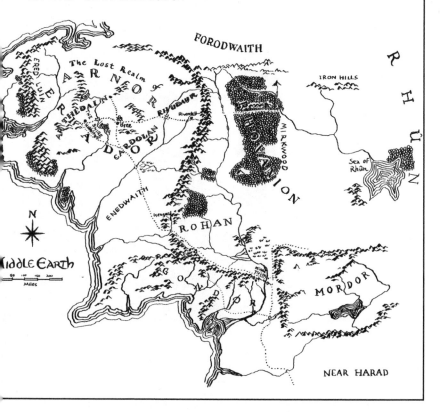

Chapter 9
Book Pirates

In 1956, Ronald was sixty-four years old. The three *Lord of the Rings* books earned so much money, he could have retired from teaching. But he planned to keep working. In fact, Ronald never spent much of his new wealth on himself. He donated money to his church and bought things for his children and their families.

Ronald and Edith still lived in the same little home in Oxford.

There was no dishwasher or washing machine, and no television. They didn't own a car. Occasionally, Ronald splurged on a fancy lunch in a restaurant or a new corduroy jacket or a dress for Edith.

Allen & Unwin made plans to have the books translated and published in other countries. Of course Ronald took a great interest in all the translations, sometimes arguing with the word choices in the new books.

In 1963, Ronald got a sad shock when his old friend Jack Lewis died. He was only sixty-four. Ronald told his daughter, Priscilla, that as an older man, he'd already started to feel like a tree that was "losing all its leaves one by one." But Jack's death, he said, felt like "an axe-blow near the roots."

In America, Ace Books planned a paperback version of *The Lord of the Rings*. Ronald had not signed a contract with Ace. The books would be "unauthorized." That meant Ronald would not get any of the money they made. These books were considered "pirate" editions.

Ronald's American publisher, Houghton Mifflin, hoped to publish their own paperback editions first. But they wanted Ronald to make some changes. That way, people would be getting the very latest and best version. Ronald promised to make the changes. However, he was hard at work writing more stories, and he had more fan mail to answer than ever.

People wrote asking him for Middle-earth names for their pets, and Ronald was glad to oblige. When they asked for an explanation of something in the book, he gave them a detailed history. One man wrote just because he'd heard that he shared his name—Sam Gamgee—with one of the lead characters. Ronald sent him signed copies of all three books and explained that "gamgee" was what the people of Sarehole called cotton wool.

While Ronald was busy answering fan mail, Ace began selling their paperback editions. They were a big hit, especially among college students. The paperbacks were inexpensive but well-made and easy to carry around.

Late in 1965, Houghton Mifflin finally published *The Lord of the Rings* in paperback. The books had a printed message from Ronald asking readers to buy that version, and no other.

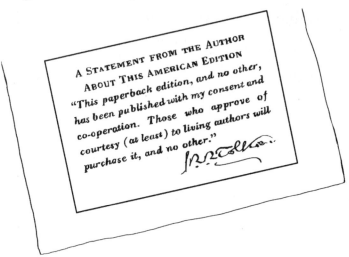

A STATEMENT FROM THE AUTHOR
ABOUT THIS AMERICAN EDITION
"This paperback edition, and no other, has been published with my consent and co-operation. Those who approve of courtesy (at least) to living authors will purchase it, and no other."
JRRTolkien.

Ronald also started to include a little note in all his letters to American fans. He explained that he made no money off the Ace editions, so could they please ask their friends to buy the other ones?

Ronald's letter writing, which had so interfered with his getting things done, now worked in his favor. His American fans truly appreciated the care and effort he put into writing to them. He'd become like a friend to his readers. His fans now sprang to his defense, protesting the Ace books. They were so insistent, Ace not only stopped publishing their editions but also paid Ronald for all the books they'd sold. The "pirates" had been defeated!

Chapter 10
Frodo Lives

US college students in the 1960s knew that Tolkien's books were about more than just wizards and dragons. The "counterculture" was a youth movement that started in the United States and spread throughout the world. In the 1960s, there was a large population of teenagers who had been born in the years just after World War II.

They had very different ideas from their parents about things like the Vietnam War, racial equality, and women's rights.

They experimented with drugs and had their own styles of dress and music. They read *The Lord of the Rings* and discovered a society where people were free and peaceful and loved nature. Young environmentalists were inspired by the stories. They hated Sauron for trying to destroy nature.

The books were loved both by war protestors *and* by many of the soldiers fighting in Vietnam. The mysterious phrase *Frodo Lives!* started to

appear written on walls, and then on buttons and bumper stickers. It meant that Ronald's characters and his world were alive in the imaginations of readers. Ronald didn't quite understand his new fans. He was old enough to be the grandfather of many of these young people with their long hair and strange clothes. But he was glad they loved his stories.

In 1966, Edith and Ronald celebrated their fiftieth wedding anniversary. Over the years, Edith had developed arthritis. It was hard for her walk up the stairs of the house.

When Ronald retired from teaching, he and Edith moved to Bournemouth, a resort town near the sea.

Bournemouth was not the type of place that Ronald liked. However, he felt that Edith had spent her whole life at Oxford for him. Now it was his turn to live where she wanted to be.

Edith made a lot of friends in Bournemouth. Ronald continued to work on new stories about Middle-earth.

In November 1971, Edith was rushed to the hospital with an inflamed gallbladder. She died days later on November 29. She was eighty-two. Ronald had loved her since he was sixteen years old. There was no reason for him to stay in Bournemouth without Edith, so he returned to Oxford.

He spent a lot of time with Christopher, who now taught at Oxford just as his father had. Ronald often visited his daughter, Priscilla, and his old friend Christopher Wiseman. He spent a few weeks with John, who was now a priest, and the two visited Hilary together. He also spent time

with Michael. On Sundays he visited Edith's grave
in the Catholic section of Wolvercote Cemetery in
Oxford.

Many American universities asked Ronald
to visit, but he felt too old to journey to the
United States. He did accept an invitation to
Buckingham Palace. Queen Elizabeth herself
awarded him a CBE (Commander of the Order
of the British Empire) on March 28, 1972.

That same year, Oxford presented him with an honorary Doctorate of Letters. This honor perhaps meant the most to him, because it was the only one he received that wasn't for *The Lord of the Rings*. It was for his work in the study of historical languages.

Through it all, Ronald was still writing, usually with Christopher's help.

In August 1973, Ronald traveled back to Bournemouth to visit with some friends. While there, he was diagnosed with an ulcer and then a chest infection. Michael and Christopher were both out of the country, but John and Priscilla came to be with him. He died on September 2, 1973. He was eighty-one.

Ronald was buried beside Edith in Oxford. The single gravestone reads: EDITH MARY TOLKIEN, LUTHIEN; JOHN RONALD REUEL TOLKIEN, BEREN. Ronald had chosen the names of the mortal man and the immortal elven princess who fell in love to mark his and Edith's final resting place.

After his father's death, Christopher continued Ronald's work. In 1977, *The Silmarillion* was finally published. It describes more of the history of Tolkien's world, including Middle-earth, where *The Hobbit* and *The Lord of the Rings* take place. In 2014, Christopher published a translation of *Beowulf* that his father had worked on for years without many people even knowing he was doing it.

Ronald Tolkien not only created his own world, he also changed ours. Today, fantasy adventures are not only for children. Epic fantasy series like Star Wars would not exist without Ronald leading the way. Role-playing games like *Dungeons & Dragons* also have their origins in Ronald's world.

He inspired other writers of fantastic stories to describe their worlds in glorious detail, inventing new words, new languages, and new histories. He encouraged readers to journey deep into their imaginations and to create their own magical, enchanting worlds.

MOVIE VERSIONS

WHEN RONALD SOLD THE RIGHTS TO MAKE MOVIES OF HIS BOOKS, HE HOPED FOR ONE OF TWO THINGS: "CASH OR KUDOS." IN OTHER WORDS, HE FELT THAT HE WOULD MAKE A LOT OF MONEY, OR THE MOVIES WOULD BE GREAT. HE DIDN'T THINK BOTH WERE POSSIBLE.

AND FOR A LONG TIME, THE SECOND IDEA SEEMED IMPOSSIBLE. THERE WERE ANIMATED VERSIONS OF BOTH *THE HOBBIT* AND *THE LORD OF THE RINGS*, BUT NONE OF THEM LIVED UP TO THE GREATNESS OF THE BOOKS.

THEN IN 2001, NEW ZEALAND DIRECTOR PETER JACKSON'S *THE FELLOWSHIP OF THE RING* WAS RELEASED. JACKSON AND HIS CAST AND CREW HAD SPENT FIFTEEN MONTHS FILMING ALL THREE MOVIES. ONE FILM A YEAR WOULD BE RELEASED FOR THREE YEARS. USING A

COMBINATION OF OLD-FASHIONED TRICKS (LIKE
HAVING THE ACTORS KNEEL SO THAT THEY WOULD
APPEAR MORE HOBBIT-SIZE) AND CUTTING-EDGE
SPECIAL EFFECTS, JACKSON GOT CLOSER THAN
ANYONE DREAMED TO BRINGING RONALD'S WORLD
TO LIFE. EVEN MORE IMPORTANT, HIS CHOSEN
CAST REALLY SEEMED TO *BE* THE CHARACTERS
THEY PLAYED. IN 2012, JACKSON RETURNED TO
MIDDLE-EARTH—ALONG WITH MANY ACTORS FROM
THE ORIGINAL FILMS—TO MAKE *THE HOBBIT.*

TIMELINE OF
J. R. R. TOLKIEN'S LIFE

1892 —— John Ronald Reuel Tolkien is born in Bloemfontein, South Africa

1896 —— Ronald's father, Arthur Tolkien, dies

1900 —— Ronald's mother, Mabel Tolkien, converts to Catholicism

1904 —— Mother dies

1908 —— Meets Edith Bratt

1916 —— Fights in the Battle of the Somme

1920 —— Becomes a professor at Leeds University

1926 —— Tolkien family moves to Oxford

1937 —— *The Hobbit* is published

1942 —— Warehouse containing copies of *The Hobbit* is destroyed by a bomb

1947 —— Rayner Unwin reads *The Lord of the Rings*

1954 —— *The Fellowship of the Ring* and *The Two Towers* are published

1955 —— *The Return of the King* is published

1959 —— Retires from teaching

1971 —— Edith Tolkien dies

1973 —— John Ronald Reuel Tolkien dies

1977 —— *The Silmarillion* is published

TIMELINE OF
THE WORLD

Ellis Island opens to immigrants in New York — **1892**

World's largest diamond, Cullinan diamond, — **1905**
is found in South Africa

Electric washer is introduced — **1907**

Boy Scouts of America is founded — **1910**

Orville Wright sets record by staying in the air — **1911**
in a glider for nine minutes and forty-five seconds

World War I begins in Europe — **1914**

The Great Gatsby by F. Scott Fitzgerald is published — **1925**

King Kong premieres at Radio City Music Hall — **1933**
in New York City

Vesuvius erupts in Italy — **1944**

Prince Rainier III becomes the ruler of Monaco — **1949**

John F. Kennedy is assassinated — **1963**
on the same day C. S. Lewis dies

First Earth Day celebrated internationally — **1970**

The Return of the King wins the — **2004**
Academy Award for Best Picture

BIBLIOGRAPHY

Acocella, Joan. "Slaying Monsters: Tolkien's *Beowulf*." **The New Yorker**. June 2, 2014.

Carpenter, Humphrey. **J. R. R. Tolkien: A Biography**. Boston: Houghton Mifflin, 1987. First published 1977.

Carpenter, Humphrey. **The Inklings: C. S. Lewis, J. R. R. Tolkien, Charles Williams, and Their Friends**. New York: Ballantine Books, 1981.

* Collins, David R. **J. R. R. Tolkien: Master of Fantasy**. Minneapolis, MN: Lerner Publications Co., 1992.

Duriez, Colin. **J. R. R. Tolkien: The Making of a Legend**. Oxford: Lion, 2012.

Hammond, Wayne G., and Scull, Christina. **J. R. R. Tolkien: Artist & Illustrator**. Boston: Houghton Mifflin, 1995.

Neimark, Anne E. **Mythmaker: The Life of J. R. R. Tolkien, Creator of _The Hobbit_ and _The Lord of the Rings_**. Boston: Harcourt Children's Books: Houghton Mifflin Harcourt, 2012.

Pearce, Joseph. **Tolkien: Man and Myth**. San Francisco: Ignatius Press, 1998.

Ready, William. **Understanding Tolkien and _The Lord of the Rings_**. Original title: **The Tolkien Relation**. New York: Warner, 1969.

Shippey, Tom. **J. R. R. Tolkien: Author of the Century**. Boston: Houghton Mifflin, 2001.

Tyler, J. E. A. **The Tolkien Companion**. New York: St. Martin's Press, 1976.

* Wallner, Alexandra. **J. R. R. Tolkien**. New York: Holiday House, 2011.

* Books for young readers